empower

publishing

God's Littlest Miracle

Dianne Nicholas Goodrich

Illustrated by Jordan Nicholas

empower

publishing

Empower Books
PO Box 26701
Winston-Salem, NC 27114

First Empower Books edition published
December, 2019

Empower Books, Moon Sailor, and all production design are trademarks of Indigo Sea Press, used under license.

Dianne Nicholas Goodrich, Author
Jordan Nicholas, Illustrator at
Jodesigns.pb.design

Edited and Interior Layout Design by Dr. Linda Fox Felker, at Felker Consulting, Inc., Winston-Salem, NC 27103

Manufactured in the United States America
ISBN 978-1-63066-497-8

Sunday School and church services were over, and Mr. Tim was talking with his friends.

Mrs. Brewer came up and asked Mr. Tim if he would trim the bushes at her house.

Mr. Tim said, "Yes," he would trim the bushes at Mrs. Brewer's house.

Two weeks later, Mr. Tim put the tools
he needed to cut the bushes in his car
and drove to Mrs. Brewer's house.

He took his hedge clippers out of the car
and talked to Mrs. Brewer.

"It is a beautiful day to work in the yard."
he said.

They talked about all the work that needed
to be done and Mr. Tim was ready to begin.

As Tim started to trim the bushes, he noticed there were dark clouds forming in the sky.

Mr. Tim knew he would need to hurry because it looked like a bad storm was heading toward them.

He scurried about trying to finish the job before the storm began.

By then, the clouds were

moving in the sky and heading

in a different direction.

He finished his work trimming the bushes around the house, and Mrs. Brewer paid him for a job well done.

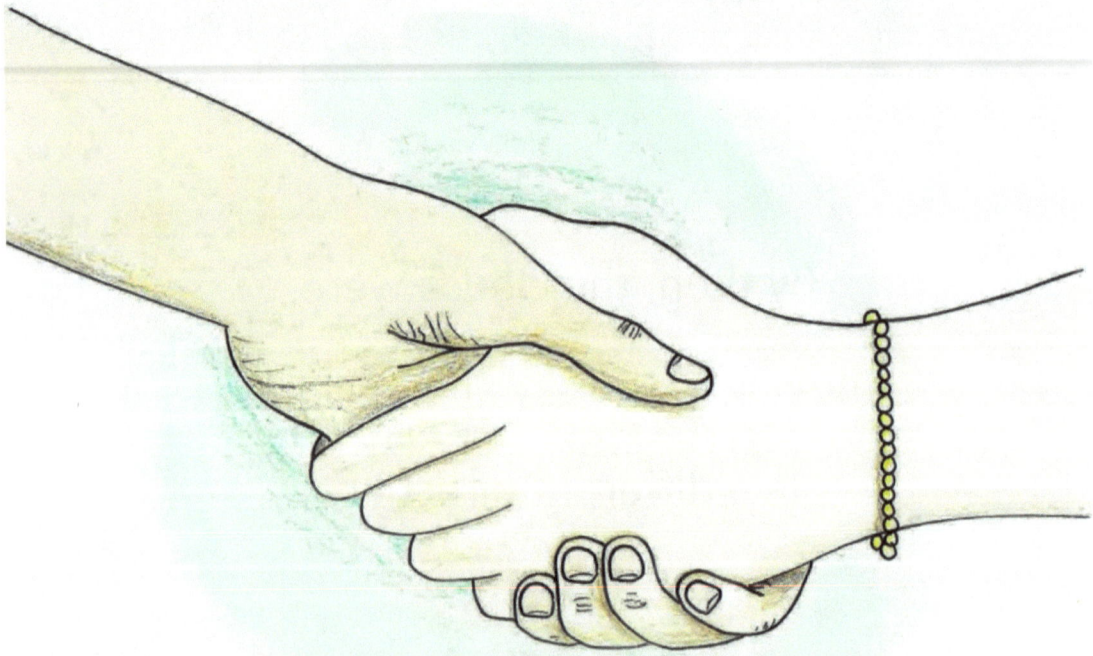

The next day, Mr. Tim's wife received a phone call from Mrs. Brewer.

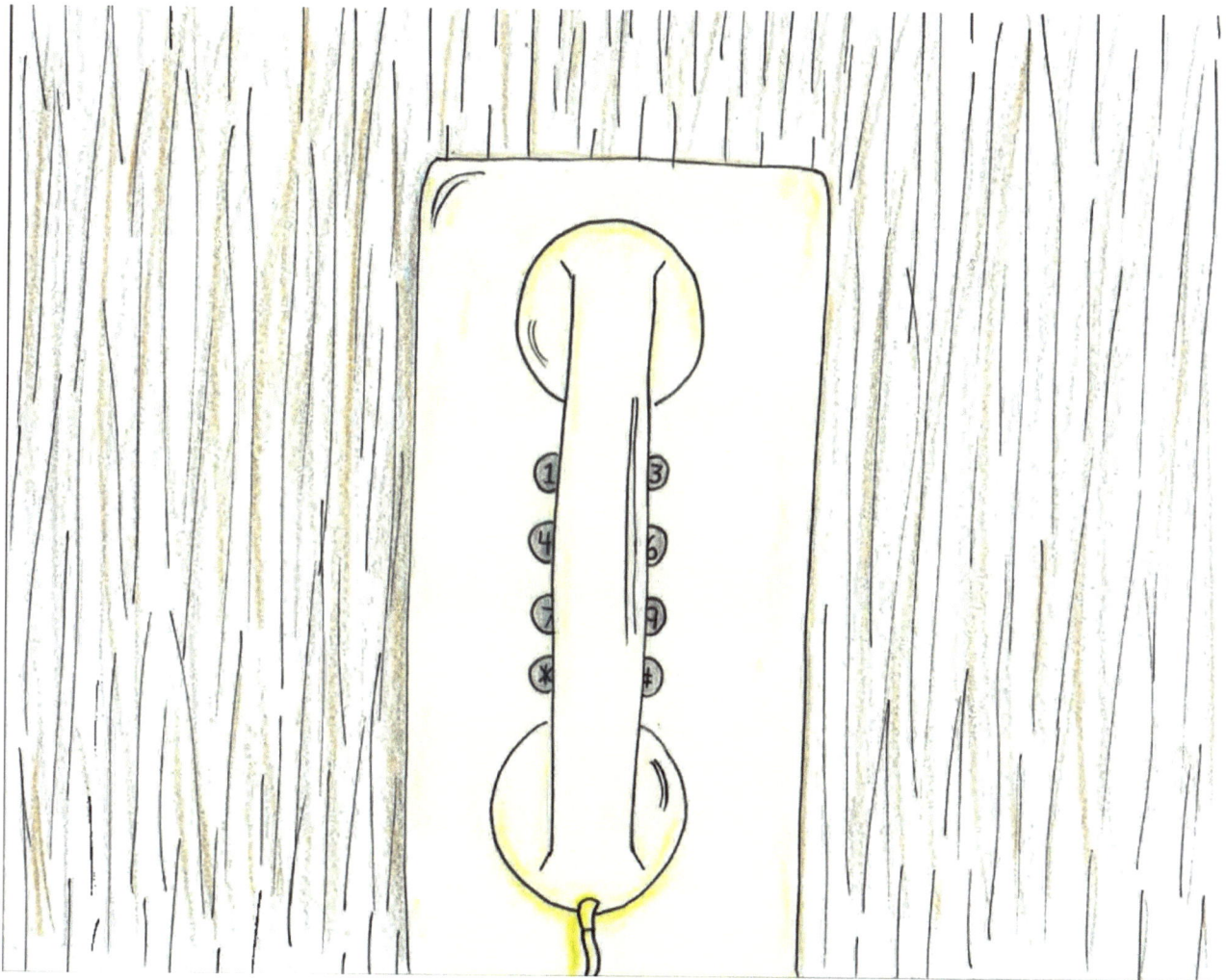

Mrs. Brewer started to talk in an excited voice about a miracle that happened at her house.

Mrs. Brewer said that all the bushes that Mr. Tim trimmed were very shapely, except for one bush beside the carport.

That bush had been left uneven. Then, she saw that there was a bird nest and a bird inside the bush.

As they talked, they believed that, if the bush had been trimmed evenly, the nest would have been destroyed and the baby bird would have been killed.

Later that evening, Mr. Tim's wife explained the miracle that happened. She told Mr. Tim the story.

He remembered what God's Word says about the sparrow in Matthew 10:29-30.

The Bible says God knows when a sparrow falls and that He cares about even the smallest bird and animals He created.

If God cares for them, just think how much more God cares for us!

His love and care for us is much greater!
God loves us so much that He sent His only
begotten Son, Jesus, to die on the cross for
our sins!

Three days later, Jesus arose from the grave
and went to Heaven to be with God, His
Father.

John 3:16 says, "For God so loved the world that He gave his only begotten Son, that whosoever believeth in Him should not perish but have everlasting life."

God loved that little bird in the bush, but God loves you even more!

About the Author

Dianne Nicholas Goodrich was born in Hampton, Virginia. She taught and worked with young children for over 28 years.

She and her husband, Timothy W. Goodrich, have been married for 45 years. They have two grown children, a son Stephen, and a daughter, Mary Beth. They also have three grandchildren, Gracyn, Waylon, and Keeley.

Dianne and Tim still enjoy teaching students in a Christian school in Lexington, NC. They are members of Sheets Memorial Baptist Church.

Dedication

This book is dedicated to my Mom and Dad. During their lives, they were a great and Godly influence on me.

I also dedicate this book to Tim, my loving and supportive husband.

Most of all, I am thankful to my Lord and Savior, Jesus Christ.